D0893638

# MARIE CURIE

Troll Associates

# MARIE CURIE

by Louis Sabin

Illustrated by Allan Eitzen

## Troll Associates

*Library of Congress Cataloging in Publication Data*

Sabin, Louis.
   Marie Curie.

   Summary: A biography of the Polish-born scientist who,
with her husband, was awarded the 1903 Nobel Prize for
discovering radium.
   1. Curie, Marie, 1867-1934—Juvenile literature.
2. Chemists—Poland—Biography—Juvenile literature.
[1. Curie, Marie, 1867-1934.  2. Chemists]  I. Eitzen,
Allan, ill.  II. Title.
QD22.C8S23    1984    530´.092´4 [B] [92]    84-2654
ISBN 0-8167-0162-8 (lib. bdg.)
ISBN 0-8167-0163-6 (pbk.)

It was a cold winter day in the city of Paris, France. Although the sun shone brightly on the old buildings, a strong wind blew through the streets. Along these streets, a young woman quickly walked. She hardly noticed the colorful shop windows or the other people in the street. She was hurrying to her laboratory at the Sorbonne, the famous French university.

This young woman was the scientist Marie Curie. Her experiments in physics and chemistry were to change the course of scientific history. And although fame and many honors would someday be hers, she later wrote that her happiest hours had been spent in the old, drafty lab, where she carried out her experiments.

Madame Marie Curie was born in Poland in 1867. As a young girl, her name was Manya Sklodowska, and she was the youngest of five children. Her parents were teachers, and all their children were good students, so little Manya was surrounded by books and studies from the beginning.

Imagine her parents' surprise when one day Manya grabbed a book from her older sister's hands and began to read aloud! All by herself, Manya had learned to read, for she was still too young to go to school. Intrigued by the many books in the family library, she had set out to solve the mystery of their words and letters.

It was this same curiosity that later led Manya to tackle some of the most challenging scientific questions of the nineteenth and twentieth centuries.

While a student at the Sorbonne, Manya, who had changed her name to the French "Marie," studied chemistry and mathematics. At the university, she learned of the work of the French scientist Henri Becquerel. Becquerel had studied a substance called uranium. He found that uranium gave off mysterious rays that could pass through air and even through solid materials. He also noticed that when he placed the uranium in the dark, it gave off a strange glow.

Marie was puzzled by these mysterious rays. After she completed her work in math and science, she decided to do further studies—she would find out about the rays discovered by Becquerel!

As a student, Marie spent most of her time reading and studying. She was very poor and often ate only bread, butter, and tea for weeks at a time. In fact, she sometimes became so lost in her work that she even forgot to eat! But Marie did find time to meet and talk with one of the university's young science teachers—Pierre Curie. Pierre was a quiet person, but with Marie he forgot his shyness. Together they would talk of science and the discoveries they hoped to make.

In 1895, Pierre and Marie were married. On their honeymoon, they set off on bicycles to tour the French countryside. They returned to Paris happy and refreshed—and ready to begin their work on Becquerel's rays. The Curies loved one another deeply, but their marriage was more than that. It was the beginning of a most remarkable scientific partnership.

In an old shed, the Curies set up their laboratory. Marie hoped to find out what caused the rays given off by uranium. She thought that the rays coming from uranium should be given a name, so she used the name *radioactivity*—a name that is still used today.

In her lab, Marie had a machine that measured the amount of rays given off by uranium and other substances. One of these other substances was *pitchblende*, a dark, soil-like metal ore, in which uranium is found. As Marie measured the radioactivity of the pitchblende, she found something very strange: the pitchblende was giving off many more rays than was the pure uranium.

This meant that the pitchblende must contain an element other than uranium that was also radioactive. But none of the other elements known at that time were radioactive. Marie grew more excited—could it be that the substance giving off the rays was a completely new element?

Marie realized how important such a finding would be. It would cause great excitement among the world's scientists, who at that time believed that all the materials found on earth were made up of combinations of seventy-four different elements. They thought of these elements as the building blocks of nature.

Marie explained her idea to Pierre, and he agreed that they were on the verge of an important discovery. But the Curies also knew that in the world of science, a theory, or idea, is not enough. A scientist must have proof. So together, they worked to find the new element.

To get a pure sample of the new element, the pitchblende had to be broken down into its basic elements. Imagine you were given a loaf of bread made up of flour, milk, and eggs, and someone asked you to take a cup and fill it with the flour that is in the bread. The Curies' problem was much the same.

In huge vats, Pierre and Marie boiled down the pitchblende, constantly stirring it with a large iron bar. Then they ground up the remaining substances and treated them with chemicals to break them down even more.

To see if they had a pure sample of the new element, they conducted tests. Carefully, they recorded the results of their experiments in a notebook. It was an exhausting task, but the Curies worked tirelessly. They broke down over a ton of pitchblende to get less than a thimble full of the new element.

Finally, after four long and discouraging years, proof of their theory was found! They discovered that the pitchblende contained not one, but two new elements. The Curies named these radioactive elements *polonium* and *radium*.

For their achievement, Marie and Pierre were awarded the Nobel prize, one of the highest honors given for scientific discovery. Marie Curie was the first woman ever to receive this prize.

The Curies continued their work. They studied the waves and the glow given off by radium, and they looked for possible uses for their new elements.

In 1906, while at the height of their fame, misfortune struck. Pierre was run down and killed in a street accident. For Marie, the tragedy was a turning point. She mourned the loss of her husband by throwing herself completely into her work. She took over Pierre's teaching position at the university, carrying on his work and theories. She also continued to study radium.

Marie Curie received another Nobel prize in 1911. In her acceptance speech, Marie shared credit for all her discoveries with her beloved Pierre.

Marie used the money from her Nobel prizes unselfishly. She set up science scholarships and helped to establish a center for the study of medical uses for radium. During World War I, she contributed money to the French government to help buy the weapons needed to defend France.

But her contribution to France during the war was more than a donation of money. Marie also gave of her time and scientific skills. From her study of radioactivity, Marie knew about another kind of ray called an x ray. It could be used to look inside the human body to find broken bones or other wounds.

Marie and her daughter, Irène, created an x-ray clinic that could be moved from battlefield to battlefield. They took their traveling clinic to the front lines of the war, treating thousands of wounded soldiers.

After the war, Marie Curie remained active, despite ill health. She worked with her daughter and son-in-law on many important experiments.

Madame Curie also set up and helped to run two radium clinics—one in Poland and one in France. Marie believed that scientists of all nations would be better able to understand one another's work if everyone used the same scientific symbols and terms. As a member of many science committees throughout the world, she worked very hard to achieve this goal.

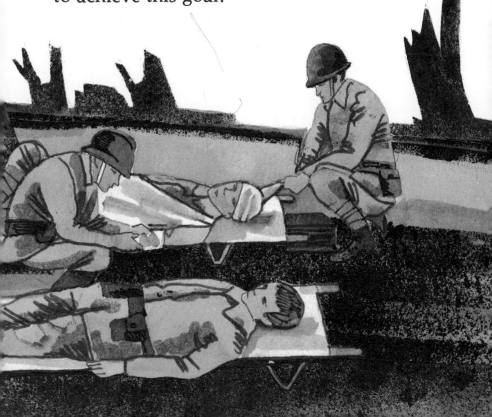

The discoveries of Marie and Pierre Curie contributed greatly to science. Their studies led to our present understanding of the structure of atoms, the tiny particles that make up each element. Today, scientists are still discovering uses for radium and other radioactive materials.

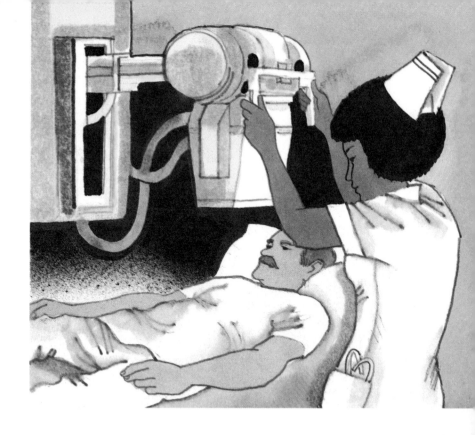

Perhaps radium's most important use is in the practice of medicine, for the rays given off by radium are helpful in treating cancer. But sadly, the same substance that is now used as a cure was also the cause of Madame Curie's death. Her long hours in the lab had put her in contact with dangerously large amounts of radioactivity, which resulted in her death in 1934. But without her work, radium's helpful effects might never have been realized.

Today, as we build upon the genius and hard work of Marie and Pierre Curie, our knowledge of the world grows.